Up, Up and Away

Hello!

BRIDGEND

Edited by Simon Harwin

First published in Great Britain in 2000 by
YOUNG WRITERS
Remus House,
Coltsfoot Drive,
Peterborough, PE2 9JX
Telephone (01733) 890066

HB ISBN 0 75432 256 4
SB ISBN 0 75432 257 2

FOREWORD

This year, the Young Writers' Up, Up & Away competition proudly presents a showcase of the best poetic talent from over 70,000 up-and-coming writers nationwide.

Successful in continuing our aim of promoting writing and creativity in children, our regional anthologies give a vivid insight into the thoughts, emotions and experiences of today's younger generation, displaying their inventive writing in its originality.

The thought, effort, imagination and hard work put into each poem impressed us all and again the task of editing proved challenging due to the quality of entries received, but was nevertheless enjoyable. We hope you are as pleased as we are with the final selection and that you continue to enjoy *Up, Up & Away Bridgend* for many years to come.

CONTENTS

Sam Lewis   34
Melody Johns   35
Luke Webber   36
Lucy Phipps   37
Kirsty Thomas   38
Dena Harris   39
Adam Quantock   40
Tara Bryne   41

Oldcastle Junior School

Amy Aitken   42
Ellie Langford   43
Lowri Pritchard   44
Sam Bailey   45
Hannah Evans   46
Corinne Lee   47
Robert Harper   48
Katherine Queenan   49
Matthew Woodroff   50
Hywel Robinson   51
Anisha Govani   52
John Llewelyn Nicholas   53
Cai Loughran   54
Phoebe Hathaway   55
Paris Williams   56
Jay Toor   57
Alyn Hawke   58
Jenna Yardley   59
Elliot Lugg   60
Christopher Tough   61
William Slade   62
Rebecca Manning-James   63
Jodie Langford   64
Emma Whiteley   65
Thomas Williams   66
Danielle Burnell   67
Kimberley Payne   68
Ross Allen   69

Emily Fisher	70
Amée Hunt	71
Megan Apsee	72
Kim Harris	73
Gemma David	74
Laura Handley	75
Sarah Blackall	76
Ellis Davies	77
Ella Desmond-Williams	78
Suzanne Beynon	79
Philip Brooks	80
Thomas Lloyd	81
Rebecca Cooper	82
Leanne Hughes	83
Anghard Hobby	84
Ruth Felton	85
Joe Eller	86
Joanna Plow	87
Briony Phillips	88
Sam Beard	89
Christopher Lynch	90
Taylor Morgan	91
Samantha James	92
Chelsey Gillard	93
Adrienne Barr	94
David Kalinka	95
Daniel Allen	96
Sian Roberts	97

Pen Y Fai CIW Primary School

Jessica Pugh	98
Adam Conybeare	99
Jessica Coombes	100
Jack Lewis	101
Matthew Hof	102
Rhian Jordan	103
Ceri Philpott	104
Mark Borgia	105

The Poems

THE WHALE

Enormous
Swimming mammal
Under the sea,
Tail fins splashing high.
Amazing.

Huw Royal (9)
Blaengarw Primary School

OLLY THE OSTRICH

Olly the ostrich
Is wild and free
He's the strangest bird
You'll ever see.
He's got long, thin legs
And a long, scrawny neck,
A short, tough beak
That can give a nasty peck.
He's not very brave
Although he's the biggest bird on land
If he gets a fright
He'll bury his head in the sand.

Ashley Williams (8)
Blaengarw Primary School

CRAIG THE CAT

Craig the cat
Sleeps with one eye open
Watching for mice
For a snack he is hoping.
He prowls around the garden
In the shadow of the night
Watching and waiting
To give a mouse a fright.
He sleeps by day
In a spot in the sun
Purring and dreaming
Of the hunting he has done.
Craig the cat
Sleeps with one eye open
Watching for mice
For a snack he is hoping.

Craig Rogers (8)
Blaengarw Primary School

LAUREN THE LION

Lauren the lion
Is a big, fierce cat
She's frightening and scary
But she doesn't like that.

She wants to be gentle
She wants to have friends
She'd like to go to parties
And bring pals back to her den.

Lauren the lion
Is a big, fierce cat
She's frightening and scary
But she doesn't like that.

Lauren McEachen (8)
Blaengarw Primary School

LIAM THE LEOPARD

Liam the leopard
Is covered in spots
He looks like he's caught chicken pox
He's blotchy and spotty
With patches and dots
If you need a counter
He's got lots and lots
He lives in a jungle
Where he hides in the shade
Watching and waiting
To pounce on his prey
Liam the leopard
Is covered in spots
He looks like he's caught
Chicken pox.

Liam Ward (8)
Blaengarw Primary School

ELERI THE ELEPHANT

Eleri the elephant
Has a long grey trunk
Great big ears
She's a big grey lump.

She lives in a jungle
Where she likes to play
But she'd like to change her colour
To look more exciting than grey.

She'd like to be a mixture
Of purple, pink and blue
She thinks she'll look much prettier
Than other elephants do.

Eleri Rowling (8)
Blaengarw Primary School

JAY THE JAGUAR

Jay the jaguar he is king
Of the lush, green forest
Where hummingbirds sing.
He's fast and powerful
With sharp, strong teeth.
His claws are vicious as he tears through meat
He watches from a shady tree
At all who work below.
If he's feeling hungry
His temper you will know.
He strikes as fast as lightning
You'll have no chance to run.
Sharing his jungle home
Is certainly no fun.
Jay the jaguar he is king
Of the lush, green forest
Where hummingbirds sing.

Rhys Fisher (8)
Blaengarw Primary School

CHRISTMAS IS LIKE A . . .

Christmas is like a shout of joy,
Christmas is like a happy day.
Christmas is like a birthday party.

A star is like a piece of broken glass,
A star is like a golden light.
A star is like a shiny coin.

A baby is like a pink marshmallow,
A baby is like a new beginner.
A baby is like a pink, fluffy cloud.

Snow is like a soft, white carpet,
Snow is like a white football.
Snow is like a soft toy.

Steven Andrew Wood (8)
Blaengarw Primary School

MR FOX

He's sly and cunning,
With wicked eyes
And a coat lie a flaming fire.
Beware of Mr Fox.

He's sly and cunning
With teeth like a saw blade
And a tail like a brush.
Beware of Mr Fox.

He's sly and cunning
With ears as good as bats'
And legs that run as fast as lightning.
Beware of Mr Fox.

Ross Day (8)
Blaengarw Primary School

Mr Fox

He's sly and cunning
With big, sharp eyes
And a fluffy tail.
Beware of Mr Fox.

He's sly and cunning
With dark, beady eyes
And a long, bushy tail
Beware of Mr Fox.

Callum Burroughs (8)
Blaengarw Primary School

Magical Millennium

Magical, mystical from 1999 we part,
It's a new millennium which means a fresh start,
Lovely fireworks make the sky bright,
Luxurious lights in the dark night.
Everlasting memories live for this day.
Number changing on the dates,
Nothing can stand in time's way.
I promise to help my family more
Unlike last year which was a bore.
Magical, mystical, a night to remember.

Jonathan Jones (10)
Blaengarw Primary School

I WANNA BE . . .

I wanna be a spy,
I wanna be a private eye,
I wanna be unable to die,
I said 'Yeah, yeah, yeah,
I wanna be a spy.'

I wanna be a dog,
I wanna chase mogs,
I wanna run around and jump on logs,
I said 'Yeah, yeah, yeah,
I wanna be a dog.'

I wanna be an eye,
I wanna look into the sky,
I wanna see the birds fly,
I said 'Yeah, yeah, yeah,
I wanna be an eye.'

I wanna be a spy,
I wanna be a spy,
But really now I am telling you a lie.

Kyle Galtry (11)
Blaengarw Primary School

MILLENNIUM

M illennium Bugs coming and going
I magine things glistening and glowing
L ights are bursting in the sky
L earning new things in the new year
E verybody eating party food
N ew year is coming soon
N ew resolutions being made
I hope I can keep mine
U nbelievable fireworks
M y resolution is that I will tidy my bedroom.

Sarah Read (9)
Blaengarw Primary School

I WANNA BE . . .

I wanna be a superstar
I wanna go very far,
I wanna buy a brand new car
I said 'Yeah, yeah, yeah,
I wanna be a superstar.'

I wanna be a mighty sun
I wanna be turned into a big bun
I said 'Yeah, yeah, yeah,
I wanna be a mighty sun.'

I wanna be a millionaire
I wanna travel everywhere
I wanna care for everyone
I said 'Yeah, yeah, yeah,
I wanna be a millionaire.'

I wanna be a superstar
I wanna be a superstar
But, I can't because I'm too young
I'm only allowed to school so far.

Lyndsay Jade Larkin (10)
Blaengarw Primary School

THE MARROG

M ysterious,mean monster
A ngry aliens, horrid, sharp
R agged, roaring, ugly monster
R eally deadly devil
O ctopus arms and horrid head
G o to the class and you will tremble with fear.

Sarah Brimble (9)
Blaengarw Primary School

I WANNA BE . . .

I wanna be a football star
I wanna play far
I wanna go to football in my huge yellow car
I said 'Yeah, yeah, yeah
I wanna be a football star.'

I wanna be a sun
I wanna eat a bun
I wanna weigh a ton
I said 'Yeah, yeah, yeah
I wanna be a sun.'

I wanna be a grain of rice
I wanna be nice
I wanna eat a block of ice
I said 'Yeah, yeah, yeah
I wanna be a grain of rice.'

I wanna be a pint of beer
I wanna be near
I wanna catch a tear
I said 'Yeah, yeah, yeah
I wanna be a pint of beer.'

I wanna be a star
I wanna be a star
But I only got a job behind a bar -
So far.

Paul Ward (11)
Blaengarw Primary School

THE MARROG

T errifying, tall, frightening marrog,
H ideous monster, stamping around,
E ating, munching, horrid monster.

M onstrous, mighty brass body,
A rguing, petrifying monster, you can tell by his face
R eally I think he is from an unusual place.
R iding past the sun in his funny-shaped ship,
O h but he isn't a normal marrog, he is from Mars.
G asping, shouting, scream marrog, frightening the people looking
at the stars.

Beth Brimble (10)
Blaengarw Primary School

THE MARROG

T   all, terrifying marrog, tall as a house,
H   ideous looking marrog, getting ready to pounce,
E   normous marrog, lurking at the back of the class.

M ighty monster with a body of brass,
A   petrifying marrog with five silver arms,
R   osy teeth the marrog has, and spikes inside his palms.
R   eaches out to grab us, we all run with fear.
O n the way out we tell everyone a marrog is here.
G o away marrog, don't come back for a light year!

Rhian McEachen (10)
Blaengarw Primary School

THE MARROG

T eacher shouting all the time,
H urtful hideous brass spine
E normous at seven feet tall.

M ini spikes which are really small,
A fearless marrog is here
R eally no one is aware
R eally no one is aware
O h he's here, they'd all scream if they knew
G oing back I am right now . . . bye.

Rebecca Thomas (10)
Blaengarw Primary School

THE MARROG

T he marrog sits at the back of the class
H is tooth is sharper than a spear,
E normous with a body of brass.

'M onster' they would quiver with fear
A bloodthirsty goo.
'R oar' they'd better shoo
R aiding the town
'O h no.' Houses fall down as you can see,
G osh that marrog is me!

Stephen Whittingham (9)
Blaengarw Primary School

I Wanna Be A . . .

I wanna be a cat
I wanna chase a rat
I wanna lie on a big mat
I said 'Yeah, yeah, yeah
I wanna be a cat.'

I wanna be a rat
I wanna have a hat
I wanna be chased by a big red cat
I said 'Yeah, yeah, yeah
I wanna be a rat.'

I wanna be an astronaut
I wanna be the first boy on the moon
I wanna hold a balloon
I said 'Yeah, yeah, yeah
I wanna be an astronaut.'

I wanna be a football player
I wanna be a football player
But I've only got a job as a bricklayer.

Nathan Evans (10)
Blaengarw Primary School

MILLENNIUM

M y New Year's promise is to help my mother
I n the new millennium there will be lots of cheer
L ight and dark skies welcome the millennium
L ots of fireworks went up
E ndless parties through the night
N ight-time fireworks shot into the air
N ight-time karaokes last for hours
I n the night the countdown begins
U p the clock the hands travel, closing in on twelve
M illenniums must be treasured forever.

Jonathan Alan Wood (10)
Blaengarw Primary School

WALES

W ales is a really nice place
A ll of my friends are nice
L ots of people wear leeks
E verybody is friendly
S ometimes people wear daffodils.

Katie John (7)
Nantymoel Primary School

WHAT AM I?

Four big stompers,
Lots of crushers,
Two big blinkers,
Lots of ticklers,
One long swisher,
One brown furry collar,
One loud roar.

John Lloyd (7)
Nantymoel Primary School

WHAT AM I?

One white, bushy ball
Two blue starers
Eight grey spikes
Four tiny fiddlers
Twenty sharp scratchers
Long silky shine.

Hannah Jones (8)
Nantymoel Primary School

WALES

W ales is a happy place to be
A ll the people wear leeks on St David's Day
L ots of people take part in sheep trials
E very day Wales is full of happy smiles
S ometimes people go to the countryside.

Jordan Smith (8)
Nantymoel Primary School

WALES

W ales is a wonderful place
A ll my family love Wales
L ots of friendly people live in Wales
E ating cawl
S ometimes the sun shines.

Toni Roach (8)
Nantymoel Primary School

WALES

W ales is a wonderful place to be
A nd you can play with your friends in the Wauns Park
L oving people, loving everyone
E veryone is so happy on St David's Day
S ometimes people like singing.

Charmaine Dawe (8)
Nantymoel Primary School

WHAT AM I?

One massive sniffer
One whipping wiggler
Two blue sparklers
Two huge crookers
Four stiff standers.

Amy Williams (8)
Nantymoel Primary School

WALES

W elsh ladies all around Wales
A nother year for St David's Day
L eeks are worn to celebrate
E verything is green and yellow
S t David is remembered by people.

Melanie Morgan (8)
Nantymoel Primary School

WALES

W ales is a beautiful place to live
A ll the people are friendly
L ove is so complicated
E veryone is friendly
S ometimes Wales play rugby.

Thomas Palmer (7)
Nantymoel Primary School

WHAT AM I?

Two blue spiers,
Four little feet,
One wiggly wag,
Twenty sharp scratchers,
Lots of fluffy fur.

Emily Owen (8)
Nantymoel Primary School

DRAGON

Breathing fire
Roaring very loudly
Like a dinosaur roaring
I'd feel really, really scared
Terrified.

Sarah Wenglorz (8)
Nantymoel Primary School

DRAGON

Falling buildings
Roaring very loudly
He's got very foul breath
I feel very, very scared
Faint.

Sam Lewis (7)
Nantymoel Primary School

MY MOTHER POEM

My mother plays darts
She calls them darties
She is 39 years old
And she does not like Smarties
Her name is Judith
Her birthday's in June
She is single
And she normally gets up at noon.

Melody Johns (8)
Nantymoel Primary School

Sister Poem

My sister's name is Alice
She looks like a little angel
Her hands are like velvet
Her face is like a cherub's
Her eyes are like the blue sky
Her clothes are pink and white
She moves like a slug
I think she is lovely.

Luke Webber (9)
Nantymoel Primary School

MY FAMILY

My name is Lucy Phipps
I am eight years old
I have got blonde hair
I have got fair white skin.

My father's name is Nicholas Phipps
He has black curly hair
Dark blue eyes
He has got quite long hair.

My mother's name is Joanne Phipps
When she has parties
She always gets drunk
She does not like eating Smarties.

Lucy Phipps (9)
Nantymoel Primary School

MY FAMILY

My name is Kirsty,
I am ten years old,
I'm always getting thirsty.
I am always getting cold.

My brother has a new house,
The house is very cold,
The house is very nice,
But it is also very old.

My sister is twelve,
She is very lazy,
She is nearly thirteen,
She is also crazy.

My brother is five,
He likes playing cars,
His name is Nathan
And he likes having stars.

Kirsty Thomas (10)
Nantymoel Primary School

MY MOTHER POEM

My mother's name is Donna,
She is thirty-five years old.
She works behind the bakery,
She never gets told.

She bakes some lovely cakes,
And grills some juicy steaks,
And never makes mistakes.
My mum is real fun,
Just like a sticky bun,
But most of all I love my mum.

Dena Harris (9)
Nantymoel Primary School

MY FAMILY POEM

My name is Adam
I am nine years old
I live in a huge house
But my house is pretty cold.

I have one older brother
His name is Bradley
He likes swimming in the pool
But not in the freezing sea.

I have one best friend
He is very short and noisy
His name is Ryan Lewis
And he is very dozy.

Adam Quantock (9)
Nantymoel Primary School

MY HOUSE

I have a very big house
For seven dogs, a cat and mouse
But that's not all, there are guinea pigs
And two little rabbits who always dig.

I'll tell you their names one by one
The rabbits are Rum and Tum, they are lots of fun,
The cat is called Miss Rosie Posie
Miss Rosie Posie is very nosy.

The dogs are Dopey, Doc, Bashful, Sneezy, Sleepy, Grumpy and Happy
They play with me and my teddy, Cappy.
The mouse is called Mr Cheese
Who chats to the rabbits, carrots and peas.

The guinea pigs are Sarah and Sam
Who always jump in the baby's pram
So there you have it all in my house
Count all the animals and don't forget the mouse.

Tara Byrne (8)
Nantymoel Primary School

THE MAGIC BOX

I will put in my box
Sparkling spring water shimmering in the sunlight,
The summer's sweet smell of fruit,
The taste of a cold winter's night,
Indulged in a white suit.

I will put in my box
The beam of mysterious light,
As it smashes against a great wall of snow-capped mountains,
The atmosphere of two young lovers as they
Plight their everlasting love.
A teaspoon of the silver water from two love fountains.

I will put in my box,
The noise of a marvellous mansion,
As people arrive at their destination,
The quiet whispering of a country lane,
As people live their lives without complaint.

I will put in my box,
A second sun to light the way,
A sixth day in the month called Nay,
A third moon at an autumn noon,
All these things I will have very soon.

My box will be covered in
The starlight from Heaven,
It will be held by a pin,
And will be locked by locks numbered eleven.

I shall live in my box,
On the sunny beach at Waterloo,
By the sandy shores beside the docks,
And if anybody knew
They would be sucked in with me in my box.

Amy Aitken (10)
Oldcastle Junior School

I WISH . . .

I wish I was a mouse
So I could creep about at dawn.
I wish that my dad
would get better so he can play
Football with us.
I wish I was an angel
So I could fly up, up
In the sky.
I wish I could live
In a library so I could read
All day but when it comes
To going to sleep
I just want to
Read and read.

Ellie Langford (7)
Oldcastle Junior School

I WISH . . .

I wish I were an angel
Flying in the sky gracefully
I wish my parents' dreams would come true
So they would be very, very happy.
I wish I could see my nanny
Who came and went.
I wish I had friends who lasted
Happy and peaceful we would be.
I wish I were a princess wearing a silvery dress.

Lowri Pritchard (7)
Oldcastle Junior School

I WISH . . .

I wish I were a butterfly
Floating gracefully through the clouds.
I wish I played for Man United
In front of lots of crowds.

I wish I were a frog
Leaping through the air.
I wish I were a cat
Curled up by the fire.

I wish I were a rabbit
Cosy in its burrow.
I wish I had a little brother!

Sam Bailey (8)
Oldcastle Junior School

I WISH . . .

I wish I could be a singer
So I could sing on the TV.

I wish I could travel around the
                    world with S Club 7
So they can help me sing.

I wish I could have a brother
So my sister can play with him
         and I will not get knocked over.

I wish I could go to the King's palace
So I could be royal for a day.

I wish I could fly in a balloon
So I could go to Disneyland in Paris.

Hannah Evans (8)
Oldcastle Junior School

THE MAGIC BOX

I will put in the box,
The venom of a poisonous snake,
The first sunbeams of a new day,
The water from the first bath of a baby.

I will put in the box,
The deadly sting of a scorpion,
The soothing sigh of forgiveness,
The soft touch of a silk sari.

I will put in the box,
The green tooth of a witch,
A strand of hair from a beautiful princess,
The slither of a snake.

I will put in the box,
A white rainbow and coloured rain,
A pig with webbed feet and a duck with trotters.

My box is fashioned with the waves of the Atlantic
And coal from an ancient mine.

Its hinges are the fangs of Dracula.
The lock is a bandage from a mummy.

In my box I will ride on a shooting star
And go all around the Universe in just one day.

Corinne Lee (10)
Oldcastle Junior School

THE SEA

The sea is a gentle cat,
Small and calm,
It purrs loudly all day.
With his gentle paws and swinging tail
He covers the beach lying down, letting the sun put him to sleep.

The sea is a filthy rat,
Grey and quick,
It swims in murk all day.
With his snapping jaws and crafty eyes
He turns vicious when there's a storm about.

The sea is a violent lion,
Golden and huge.
With his magnificent teeth and hind legs to jump with,
He roars all day,
He eats boats at night.

Robert Harper (9)
Oldcastle Junior School

THE SEA

The sea is a gentle cat,
Kind and calm,
It softly purrs all day.
With his small silky paws
He plays on the shores
Day after day after day.

The sea is a small, stern rat,
Filthy and grey,
It snaps at the cliffs all day
With his tail pricked up high.
He never will die,
Nothing can stop him at play.

The sea is a ferocious lion,
Hungry and harsh.
It howls and roars all day,
With his white, foamy mane
He charges at the cliffs all day.

Katherine Queenan (9)
Oldcastle Junior School

THE SEA

The sea is a scowling cat,
Big and wild,
It sleeps on the sand all day.
With his teeth all ready to snap
He sways his tail to and fro.

The sea is a suspicious rat,
Massive and dark,
It scampers everywhere all day.
With his whiskers twitching
He looks at the moon every night.

The sea is a vicious lion,
Golden fire and ravenous.
It pounces on the beach all day,
With his great teeth and paws.
He is violent to his prey in storms.

Matthew Woodroff (9)
Oldcastle Junior School

THE SEA

The sea is a savage cat,
Huge and black,
It plays with boats all day.
With his wavy fur and watery paws
He settles in the summer just lapping
                    against the crowded shores.

The sea is a nimble rat,
Small and grey,
It eats shrimps and crabs all day.
With his streamlined body and oily whiskers
He retreats to the shore for his next meal twice a day.

The sea is a violent lion,
Great and wild,
It howls and roars all day.
With his sharp claws and active paws
He pounces on the helpless sailors.

Hywel Robinson (9)
Oldcastle Junior School

THE SEA

The sea is a white, fluffy cat,
Giant and wavy-haired,
It sits and waits for food all day.
With his claws spread and his tail up with fur on end
He waits to pounce on his next victim, man, woman, boy or girl.

The sea is a ferocious yellow-toothed rat,
Big and grey,
It scavenges around all day.
With his teeth so long and his ears pricked up
He feasts on fish, boats and us.

The sea is a fierce, violent lion,
Cruel and bad-tempered,
It slaps at you all day.
With his brilliant white teeth and his sandy body
He chases boats out to sea.

Anisha Govani (8)
Oldcastle Junior School

THE SEA

The sea is a calm cat,
Small and gentle,
It sleeps and purrs all day.
With his soft little paws
He scrams on to the shores.

The sea is a scuffling rat,
Quick and mischievous,
It eats dirty food all day.
With his teeth bright and white,
He will never die.

The sea is a fierce lion,
Big and hungry,
It pounds on the cliffs all day.
With his giant waves he never behaves,
He eats up the boat and roars.

John Llewelyn Nicholas (9)
Oldcastle Junior School

THE SEA

The sea is a scrawny cat,
All sandy and grey.
It miaows all day.
With his wet whiskers and sandy paws
He plays with the boats.

The sea is a pesky rat,
All oily and black.
It scampers around all day.
He makes sea creatures die
With oil from his body.

The sea is an inactive lion,
Drowsy and dull.
It slumbers all day.
With his heavy head
He lies on the sand.

Cai Loughran (9)
Oldcastle Junior School

THE MAGIC BOX

I will put in the box,
A rabbit racing rapidly round a racetrack,
Smoke from Great Grandad's pipe,
Wizards turning witches into worms.

I will put in the box,
A horse riding across a white beach
With its wings outstretched,
A bird flying among white clouds
With its hooves thundering.

I will put in the box,
The last bark of a Spanish dog,
And the first miaow of a Swedish cat,
Also the biggest ball I kicked.

I will put in the box,
A blue star with dazzling gems in the middle,
A brick book and a smooth hedgehog.

On my box there is a sun, star and moon;
In the corner there will be black widow spiders.
My box is made from paper chosen by my little sister.

I will live in my box with an old rusty lock.
I will be able to open it when I sing the
Welsh anthem three times.

Phoebe Hathaway (11)
Oldcastle Junior School

THE MAGIC BOX

I will put in the box,
A high mountain in Kenya,
Fire from the mouth of a dragon
And a solid gold pig.

I will put in the box,
A talking elephant with a silver tail,
An octopus with a ninth leg
And big green waves.

I will put in the box,
A voice speaking in Latin,
A low valley in Alaska,
A soprano singing on a white horse
And a cowboy riding on a stage.

My box is made from silver and gold,
The corners made from sharks' teeth.

I shall skate in my box
On the high hills of Kenya,
And dream of winning the lottery
As the sun sets.

Paris Williams (10)
Oldcastle Junior School

THE MAGIC BOX

I will put in the magic box,
A glimpse of the moon eclipsing the sun,
A sip of the coldest water from the Atlantic,
A special moment with a special person.

I will put in the box,
The scales of a fearsome cobra,
The shiny reflection of silver,
The laughter of a newborn baby.

I will put in the box,
A giant tornado, twirling around and
Repeatedly barging its way through a giant city,
All the moons and planets of the Universe,
The roar of an angry lion.

I will put in the box,
A magical wizard called Merlin,
The poisonous venom of a snake,
The bright green of the grass.

My box is made of flowing water
With the sun as hinges.

I shall play sports in my box
On the sandy golden beaches and bright green grass.

Jay Toor (10)
Oldcastle Junior School

THE MAGIC BOX

I will put in the box,
An ice-cream sundae with a cherry on top,
The roaring laugh of a giant
And the song of a blue and yellow bird.

I will put in the box,
The sound of dolphins in the Caribbean,
Menacing monkeys making a mess
And a production of 'A Midsummer Night's Dream'.

My box is made from warthogs' bones
And it's under lock and key.
Its hinges are Cayman crocodiles' teeth.

I will put in my box,
A purple panda,
An eighth day of the week
And a thirteenth month of the year.

I will trek in my box
Up the hills of Wing-a-Wong
And come back home to a winning lottery ticket!

Alyn Hawke (10)
Oldcastle Junior School

THE MAGIC BOX

I will put in my box,
The first roar of a baby lion
And the last bounce of a ball.

I will put in my box,
Four china wishes,
A white rainbow
And a multicoloured raindrop.

I will put in my box,
Three barbarians bouncing in the bath,
A silver toad
And a hungry snowman.

I will put in my box,
A snoring pig,
A cow with wings
And a bird that goes 'Moo.'

My box is fashioned with ice and gold,
Tornadoes for the corners,
Its hinges are the glowing pearls of an oyster.

I will bounce in my box on a trampoline,
And reach the sky to touch the stars
And sprinkle moondust near and far.

Jenna Yardley (10)
Oldcastle Junior School

EARLY MORNING ON SOUTHERNDOWN BEACH

Early morning
And the sun comes up,
Painting the sky
With delicate pinks and oranges,
And the wave tops sparkle
In the morning light.
The beach is deserted,
No noisy children
To disturb the silence,
Just the noise of the waves
Beating on the pebbles,
The crashing of water
As the tide rushes in.
Sitting on a boulder
I feel the spray
Brushing my face
And sense the sadness,
The loneliness of the sea.
I turn away
And climb the cliff path
Anxious to return
To the warmth of home.

Elliot Lugg (10)
Oldcastle Junior School

THE SEASON AT ST BRIDES

The treetops get scorched
In the fierce fiery sun of summer,
Almost burning the leaves away.
Then comes the soft sad breath of autumn breezes
Like a puff of smoke,
The leaves swirl and there the tree is bare,
Here comes winter with a glorious morning,
The little sparkles on the snowflakes
Gleaming at your eyes and melting at the root of your tree.
The spring is a step away from a New Year's Day,
The spring has come to the seasons at St Brides,
The tree has come out of its roots.
When I arrive every spring the warmth of the newborn
Baby tree has come.

Christopher Tough (11)
Oldcastle Junior School

THE MAGIC BOX

I will put in the box,
A beach from paradise,
A horn from a blue rhino
And a ray of the sun.

I will put in the box,
A Martian time machine with a date unknown,
A hyena's laugh
And a kangaroo's punch.

I will put in the box,
The kick of a ball in the Millennium Stadium,
A dream of a child, homeless and poor
And the noise of Rudolph to lighten it up.

I will put in the box,
A crocodile's tooth, all white and clean,
The roar of a lion,
The squeak of a mouse
And the colour of a spleen.

I will put in the box,
A shooting star,
Some king's jewels
And the first heartbeat of a baby.

My box is fashioned from gold and coal,
Its hinges are made of sherbet
And the lid is bubblegum.

I will jump in my box
To the moon
And back to a world of peace.

William Slade (10)
Oldcastle Junior School

THE MAGIC BOX

I will put in the box,
The shine of a shining star in the moonlight,
Tucked up so tightly under the dark black midnight,
The ping of a falling diamond ring
And the whisper of the wind.

I will put in the box,
The glittering colours of the rainbow
That stay up so high in the sky
And the rings that circle round Saturn.

I will put in the box,
Four silver secrets
And the word 'lilacdandie',
And the first baby's cry.

I will put in the box,
A blind man's daughter
And the cobwebs that hang on the spooky skull's eye!

I will put in the box,
The magic music of a harp
And a dolphin with wings,
And a bird with fins.

I will put in my box,
The howl of a wolf,
A witch's black cat on a broomstick
And the rattlesnake's tail that rattles nearby.

My box is a symbol of life.
The cold water of the clean, clear Atlantic
                              waves move in my box.
My box is made of silver, gold, steel.
The hinges are rubies that catch, click open and shut.

Rebecca Manning-James (10)
Oldcastle Junior School

THE MAGIC BOX

I will put in the box,
Light-blue forget-me-nots floating in a summer breeze,
A horse with wings
And a bird with hooves.

I will put in the box,
Three round, purple snowballs,
Two green floating raindrops
And a little old woman knitting on an emerald moon.

I will put in the box,
Four zigzagged zebras,
Three queens quarrelling
And two kissing kangaroos kidnapping a king.

I will put in the box,
Ten hairs of a baby lion,
The first purr of the kitten
And the last page read of a book.

I will ride in my box
On six glittering white horses
And watch an ant's birthday go by.

Jodie Langford (10)
Oldcastle Junior School

THE MAGIC BOX

I will put in the box,
Dolphins from the deep blue sea,
A real live fish with two gold tails
And a beach with golden sand.

I will put in the box,
A twenty-fifth hour and a thirteenth month,
A horse with a fifth leg
And a song sung in Chinese.

I will put in the box,
The voice of an angel,
A baby's first word
And the last cry of a dying prince.

I will put in the box,
An elephant with a mane
And a lion with a trunk,
And two wishes spoken in Japanese.

My box is fashioned from jewels and gold
With shooting stars on the lid.

In my box I shall sing and dance,
I shall take off on the back of a bird,
Then I shall be washed up
On the shore of a sandy beach.

Emma Whiteley (10)
Oldcastle Junior School

THE MAGIC BOX

I will put in the box,
The scent of a rose,
The feel of sand sieving through my fingers,
The sound of the sea swishing up on the shore.

I will put in the box,
The darkness of a cold winter's night,
The sight of an eagle,
The stripe of an elephant and the trunk of a tiger.

I will put in the box,
The speed of Concorde
And the stealth of a leopard,
The heat of the sun and the coldness of Pluto,
A bus in the air and a plane on land.

I will put in the box,
Two wishes spoken by a monkey,
A bride's face as she is getting married.

My box is fashioned from the finest platinum
And the most beautiful rocks shaped into a pyramid.
Inside there is a moon and the planet Saturn,
It is lit up with the brightest fireflies in the world.

I will put in the world and all that's in it,
I will ride the solar system on my python
And sunbathe on the sun.

Thomas Williams (11)
Oldcastle Junior School

THE MAGIC BOX

I will put in the box,
Four moons, one sun of the summer day,
An eagle with a big mouth to kill,
A spark from a burning wood
And a tip of a lion's tooth.

I will put in the box,
A bull with a rumbling, tumbling belly,
A cat with red fire eyes,
A singing dog.

I will put in the box,
A tenth planet,
A multicoloured elephant,
A smile from a lion.

I will put in the box,
The wave from the ocean,
A cowboy with a nine lives cat.

I will put in the box,
A whole street of stairs,
A tip of a pen,
A black lion,
A multicoloured boy.

Danielle Burnell (10)
Oldcastle Junior School

THE MAGIC BOX

I will put in the box,
Sixteen slithery snakes,
Twenty terrible tigers.

I will put in the box,
A yellow cat on a black beach,
An orange frog which lays in the leaping sun.

I shall ski in my box
On the hot snow in the rays of the white sun.
Down the slope and turn right,
In the coffee shop I will run.

My box is blue and green
With orange hinges.
It has moons on the lid and music
In the corners.

I will put in the box
A tenth planet,
And a purple star,
A cat that barks
And a dog that miaows.

I will put in the box,
A stupid tongue with black varnish,
And a black wind in a whirl night.

Kimberley Payne (10)
Oldcastle Junior School

THE MAGIC BOX

I will put in the box,

A rugby player, running down the wing at 60mph,
The post over 50 storeys high,
The ball sailing over the posts.

I will put in the box,

£1000 worth of chocolate and sweets,
Stacks of fantastic money
And the bang of a distant gun.

I will put in the box,

A witch with a cowboy's hat,
A cowboy with a witch's hat,
Schoolchildren learning at home.

I will put in the box,

An enormous elephant that enjoys expressions,
A dingo dog that digs down deep
And an alligator that attacked an ant.

I will put in the box,

Terrible flies and horrible injuries,
Nice activities and quiet mice,
A round plate and a patterned cup.

Ross Allen (10)
Oldcastle Junior School

THE MAGIC BOX

I will put in my box,

The taste of two Twix chocolate bars,
The love I get from my parents,
The sweet smell of fresh summer fruits.

I will put in my box,

A calf with green fur,
A taste of the true waters of Naya,
A howling eagle and a soaring gale.

I will put in my box,

A sixth finger and a second brain,
The cold of a snowman,
The warmth of a fire.

My box is fashioned
From twinkling silver water,
With beaming moons on the lid
And stars in the corners.
Its hinges are the rays of light from the sun.

I shall swim in my box
With the dolphins of Scotland,
Then dance a Scottish folk dance
In a really Scottish kilt.

Emily Fisher (11)
Oldcastle Junior School

THE MAGIC BOX

I will put in my box,

Six slimy snakes,
Ten tigers trembling
And tails of rats and mice.

I will put in my box,

A melting boy,
A dead star
And a howling eagle.

I will put in my box,

A second sun,
A tenth planet
And a fourth triplet.

I will put in my box,

The last laugh of a granny
And the first joke of a baby.

My box is yellow and bright blue
With wishes in the lid
And bright green hinges.

I shall swim in my box,
Swim miles and miles
And arrive in Egypt,
With the black sun shining on me.

Amée Hunt (11)
Oldcastle Junior School

THE MAGIC BOX

I will put in my box,

The smell of chocolate melting in a pan,
The blue of a balloon on a black night,
The sound of a child sewing.

I will put in my box,

The bang of a firework on the millennium night,
The white of a swan swimming on a lake.

I will put in my box,

A fifth season and a tenth planet,
A cat that barks and a dog that purrs.

I will put in my box,

A slimy snake and a slithery frog
And a pair of my favourite shoes.
A beggar that lives in a mansion
And the King and Queen that live on the streets.

My box is magical with stars that glow in the day
And that they are made from silver and gold.
The hinges are multicoloured with silver
For the screws.

I shall swim in my box across the Atlantic,
Then I will dive down and swim with the fish,
Then finally I will land on the sandy beaches of Australia,
Then I will rest and drift asleep.

Megan Apsee (10)
Oldcastle Junior School

THE MAGIC BOX

I will put in my box,

The sight of a swan, sitting on a stream,
The tail of the oldest cat,
The smell of the sweetest rose.

I will put in my box,

A fast snail and a slow cheetah,
The sigh of relief after a war,
A monstrous mouse and a timid bear.

I will put in my box,

A cat and dog that get along,
The last glare of Hitler,
The first laugh of a born hero.

I will put in my box,

A poor queen and a rich beggar,
13 months and ten days in a week.

My box is fashioned with gold, silver and bronze
And is magical in lots of different ways,
With secrets in one corner and lies in the other.

I shall fly in my box
In the sunny sky
And float away on a white, fluffy cloud
And drift away to sleep.

Kim Harris (11)
Oldcastle Junior School

THE MAGIC BOX

I will put in my box,

The thrash of a tiger's tail,
The blaze of a burning jungle
And an ancient golden apple.

I will put in my box,

The puddle of a melted snowman,
Coloured grass with cold lights,
A boring split and a boring maths lesson.

I will put in my box,

The dream of a lonely child,
The last laugh of an old uncle
And the first kiss of a new baby.

I will put in my box,

A 60th week of a year
And an 8th day of a week
With a 62nd second of a minute.

My box is fashioned from
The magic of a witch
And the singing of a choir.

I shall swim in my box,
Swim to the end of the sea,
Then swim back to the hot beach
Beneath the boiling sun.

Gemma David (11)
Oldcastle Junior School

THE MAGIC BOX

I will put in my box,

The swish of a soft sea on a summer's night,
A buzz of a busy bee on a blazing day,
The whip of the wailing wind.

I will put in my box,

A sun with black spots,
A sip of the bluest water from Lake Eerie,
A jumping shock from an electric eel.

I will put in my box,

Three small waves from the Atlantic Ocean,
A last ache of an old man
And a first cry of a newborn child.

I will put in my box,

A second sun with purple spots,
A cowboy hovering
And a lady riding a white horse.

My box is fashioned from gold and silver,
With stars on the lid and mysteries in the corners.
Its hinges are the points on the stars.

I shall dance in my box
On a big, huge stage,
Then dance to the moonlight
In the rays of the moon.

Laura Handley (10)
Oldcastle Junior School

THE MAGIC BOX

I will put in the box,

The smell of a seashell sitting in the shallow sea water,
The only orange of the one orchard of Oregon,
The memories of my maternal grandmother.

I will put in the box,

The most handsome ogre,
The ugliest princess.

I will put in the box,

The eighth wonder of the world,
The thirteenth month,
The fourth triplet
And the sixth sense.

I will put in the box,

A queen with tatty rags,
A beggar with fine cloaks,
A snorting dog
And a barking pig

My box is blue and yellow
With fortune telling eyes on the lid.
The corners hold fireworks that were never let off
And when you open it, it sings.

I shall swim in my box
Across the Atlantic
And wake up on a deserted sandy shore.

Sarah Blackall (10)
Oldcastle Junior School

THE MAGIC BOX

I will put in my box,

The silent sways from the South African deserts,
The soft touch of a baby's skin,
A serious smile from a sorry soldier.

I will put in my box,

A blue moon and a white sea,
A yelp from a lonely puppy,
A yellow day and a rainy sun.

I will put in my box,

The thirteenth month of the year,
A mouse with a bark,
A dog with a squeak.

I will put in my box,

The seventh ocean of the world,
The cosy feeling of Christmas.

My box will be blue like the sky
With purple flowers on the lid
And glass sides.

I shall shop in my box
In the biggest shopping city in the world.
It will all fit in my box,
And so will much more.

Ellis Davies (10)
Oldcastle Junior School

THE MAGIC BOX

I will put in the box,

The sweet song of a skylark at sunrise,
Blazing wings from butterflies in the summer,
The howl of a mountain on a wolf.

I will put in the box,

A cold door in the blazing sun,
An elephant that eats eggs in England
And knits a sweater by the sizzling hot fireside.

I will put in the box,

The talk of a laughing alligator,
The brightest day from the second Earth,
And the rumbling of a hungry planet.

I will put in the box,

Five black adders that cannot bite,
Six whispers of a wind
And the last world that has now ended.

My box will be painted with flowers
And a big, blue sea from the bottom of the Atlantic Ocean,
The lid is a dinosaur's jaws which gobble things up.

I shall skate in my box
In the great world of ice,
Then I shall sleep in my box,
In the light of the rising sun.

Ella Desmond-Williams (11)
Oldcastle Junior School

THE RUNAWAY

Up to her room the girl goes,
Tear-stained, packing her bags,
Waits till everybody is asleep,
Then slowly creeps down the stairs,
Opens the front door, steps out,
Shuts the front door
And runs down the street, through the fields,
Then farms, and stops.
Where is she?
The dark shadows make everything unfamiliar.
The girl turns around and runs
As fast as she can back to her house
And regrets everything she did,
And forgets it.

Suzanne Beynon (10)
Oldcastle Junior School

LION CUB HIDING

Where you hide,
by the wet, revolting river bank.
Where you hide,
sitting with a slight shiver up your spine.

Where you hide,
vultures circle overhead like a
roundabout in a fair,
with a blazing, cunning eye.

Where you hide,
in your worst nightmare your heart would never beat so loud,
your heart's beating like the drums of Kenya,
your brain's hypnotised from following the vulture's path.

A constellation of stars overhead reminds you of staying together,
the moon's chill increases your fear.

Where you hide,
you hear a large bang and splat,
you see and count your ribcage.

Philip Brooks (10)
Oldcastle Junior School

LION CUB HIDING

Where you hide,
in the long, swaying grass.

Where you hide,
shivering with hunger and thirst.

Where you hide,
people walk by fetching water
from the river to drink.

Where you hide,
in your lonely den without your mother,
your heart pounding like a motorbike,
your paws as cold as an ice cube.

A buzzard glides in circles peering down,
the sun shining.

Where you hide,
you hear the birds squealing as they are shot,
you hear white men pulling the trigger,
bang, life becomes death.

Thomas Lloyd (9)
Oldcastle Junior School

THE MAGIC BOX

In my box I will put,

The continent of Africa
With the dancing and singing
Of African children.

The mountains of Switzerland,
The ice of Antarctica
And some Jamaican sun.

The blood of an ancient doorway,
The creak of a dying fox,
With the chatter of a silent person
And the sight of a blind human.

A seventy sun to light the way,
A purple to end the day,
A third foot to guide the way.

Rebecca Cooper (10)
Oldcastle Junior School

THE MAGIC BOX

I will put in my box,

A swish from a whale's tail,
The wave from a clear sea,
An orange octopus
And a silver, slimy starfish.

I will put in my box,

A long lime, lemon,
A short yellow lime,
A fluffy apple
And the sting of a bee.

I will put in my box,
A thirteenth month,
A twenty-sixth hour
And a seventieth second.

I will put in my box,

The last black ant,
The first laugh of a baby
And the last sparkling star.

My box is
Covered in gold and bronze stars
And a lid made of silver dollars.

I shall swim in my box
On the highest wave
To a nice warm beach
In the sun.

Leanne Hughes (10)
Oldcastle Junior School

THE SEA

The sea is a merciless cat,
Curving and snatching,
It hisses and claws all day.
With his arching back of silky fur
He tosses the pebbles away.

The sea is a savage rat,
Chewing and crunching,
It gnaws the cliffs all day.
With his tail so wet,
He could undertow you any day.

The sea is an enraged lion,
Roaring and pawing,
It devours the ships all day.
With his flaring, thundering mouth,
He invades the shore all day.

Anghard Hobby (9)
Oldcastle Junior School

HIDING

Where you hide,
in the long, swishing grass.

Where you hide,
with the fiery sun on your soft golden back.

Where you hide
hyenas prance past laughing like madmen.
You're thirsty,
but dare not step into the dangerous world;
the hyenas come sniffing, but lose interest
and walk away.

Where you hide
in your own little world,
waiting fearfully for your mother to return,
crouching lower as a tall male lion stalks by,
watching animals come and go.
Leopards eat noisily in the tree above you
and hungry vultures await a funeral.

Where you hide
you hear your brave mother's paws padding softly
and you heave a sigh of relief.

Ruth Felton (9)
Oldcastle Junior School

HIDING

Where you hide
the grass rustles like one hundred crickets.

Where you hide
a buffalo snorts not far away.

Where you hide
a huge vulture circles above waiting for prey,
growling hyenas fight savagely over their kill,
and a slippery snake
slithers silently through the grass.

Where you hide
in your dry, dusty ditch,
your heart pounding, ears twitching,
just wanting to run away;
a roar echoes across the plain, the wildebeest run
trampling everything in their path.

Where you hide,
you hear gunshots,
a bullet whistles past your ear
and you scamper away into the hazy veldt.

Joe Eller (9)
Oldcastle Junior School

HIDING

Where you hide
in a deserted ditch of gloom.

Where you hide
the pure green grass swishes back and forth
like a cheetah's slinky tail.

Where you hide
you hear the pattering footsteps of hyenas above,
standing patiently,
waiting to rip their victims to shreds.

Where you hide
in your motionless position,
the hairs on your back stand to attention,
your eyes narrow in fear;
with a fierce bang a gunshot fills the air
and the animals flee with tremendous speed.

Where you hide
you hear a bitter yelp!
You are now all alone to fend for yourself
on this dangerous African plain.

Joanna Plow (10)
Oldcastle Junior School

HIDING

Where you hide in the jagged, sharp rocks,
Where you hide no one is there to care,
Where you hide the footsteps come,
Your death is closer.
Where you hide in your dark, black corner,
The wind flows like the sea in a storm.
Your soft, white coat glows in the dark of night,
Your head is thinking of green, fresh leaves,
The warm, soft bed where life lies.
A gun blows up like a rocket,
You go deeper in the rocky cave,
The rocks cut your flesh,
The wound is deep.
Where you hide, you hear the crunch of stones,
The sign of death.
You see him, you run, a net comes over you,
Your leg hurts, you stop, you die.

Briony Phillips (10)
Oldcastle Junior School

HIDING

In the lumpy, cool mud
you hide with a cold feeling of loneliness in your heart.

Hyenas circle the pool of mud baring their teeth threateningly.

In your mind you see your mother lying dead.
Your heart's beating like a hammer hitting an anvil.
Your head's sweating, filled with memories of your mother.

A hyena laughs and a gunshot echoes silently.
The vultures squawk and the sun burns brightly.

You hear footsteps approaching you,
Then the barrel of a gun touches your head.

You growl at a man and then you see everything go black.

Sam Beard (10)
Oldcastle Junior School

CHIVVY

Grown-ups say things like . . .
Shut up moaning,
Get out of bed,
Brush your teeth,
Get some clean clothes on,
Get those smelly socks off,
You've had them for two weeks,
Make the sandwiches,
Have some breakfast,
Go to school . . .

After school . . .
Get changed,
Fold your uniform,
Do your homework,
Tidy your room,
Have your tea,
Have a bath, you smell,
Go to bed!

Christopher Lynch (10)
Oldcastle Junior School

I Wish . . .

I wish I was a princess
And I had long, shining, yellow hair.

I wish my sister would stop crying,
So I wouldn't get the blame.

I wish there was no more school
And I could play as much as I wanted.

I wish everything was free
So I could get what I want for free.

I wish the world was made of chocolate
So I could eat and eat.

I wish I could run free with the animals.
I love them.

Taylor Morgan (8)
Oldcastle Junior School

THE SEA

The sea is a sleepy cat,
Soft and shiny,
It is yawning and dreaming all day.
With his velvet and smooth coat,
He twinkles on a sunny day.

The sea is a skittish rat,
Grey and fast,
It leaps and scratches all day.
With his ugly face and eyes
He is swishing his long tail back and forward all day.

The sea is a lively lion,
Rough and tough
It roars and growls all day.
With his sharp teeth he will bite,
He is hungry and fierce.

Samantha James (8)
Oldcastle Junior School

THE SEA

The sea is a frisky cat,
Purring and pawing,
It rolls ships playfully all day.
With glowing eyes,
He prances and dances,
All night and day.

The sea is an evil rat,
Vicious and merciless.
It schemes to trap victims all day.
With his unforgivable attitude,
He entices people away from the shore.

The sea is a savage lion,
Pouncing and roaring,
It hunts for food all day.
With his razor-sharp teeth and dangerous black claws
He devours people every day.

Chelsey Gillard (9)
Oldcastle Junior School

THE SEA

The sea is a fierce cat
hissing and clawing,
it pounces on cliffs all day.
With his rough claws he runs
down the beach.
He angrily grabs boats out at sea.

The sea is an unforgiving rat,
evil and fierce.
It makes angry noises all day.
With his tail he whips the beach,
he is mad with anger.

The sea is a ferocious lion,
killing the fish and clawing
at the cliffs.
He roars loudly all day,
with his teeth eating the sand.
He scares sailors and rocks their boats.

Adrienne Barr (8)
Oldcastle Junior School

THE SEA

The sea is a serene cat, still and calm,
He lies all day.
With his lazy paws and his tired feet
He lazes about on the sand till the break of day.

The sea is an unforgiving rat,
He scrambles and trembles,
He menaces all day.
With his evil look and his merciless brain
He cannot be trusted.

The sea is an angry lion,
He is rough and tough.
He pounces on the beach all day
With his sharp claws and his fearful face,
He is a fierce beast.

David Kalinka (8)
Oldcastle Junior School

THE SEA

The sea is a calm cat,
Sleeping and snoring,
He purrs and miaows all day.
With his tail blowing in the wind,
He just lets himself flop and turn over.

The sea is a scurrying rat,
Scuttling and darting,
He whizzes everywhere all day.
With his tail swishing into the rockpools,
He rolls over the rocks, washing away crabs and shells.

The sea is a ferocious lion,
Snarling and roaring,
He runs and pounces all day.
With his razor blade teeth
He bites and swallows ships.

Daniel Allen (9)
Oldcastle Junior School

THE SEA

The sea is a serene cat,
Stretching and purring,
He sleeps on the beach all day.
With his whiskers, he brushes the sea,
He is weary, calm and smooth.

The sea is a fierce rat,
Searching and sniffing.
He plays and bites all day.
With his thick scratching paws
He runs along the sand.
He scatters round and along the beach.

The sea is a wild lion,
Growling and fighting,
He roars and claws all day.
With his tail he whips the beach,
He viciously pounds the rocks with his paws.

Sian Roberts (9)
Oldcastle Junior School

KENNING

A funny winker,
A cool blinker,
A warm sleeper,
A flashing machine,
A coloured beam,
A water dribbler,
A small twinkler,
A sparkling ball of glitter.

An eye.

Jessica Pugh (11)
Pen Y Fai CIW Primary School

OLD TRAFFORD

It's the Theatre of Dreams,
It's a massive circle,
It's an all-seater stadium,
It's a legend,
It's a child's dream,
It's everyone's favourite place,
It's home of the Red Devils,
It's where football is played,
It's team is fantastic,
It's where everybody wants to play.

Adam Conybeare (11)
Pen Y Fai CIW Primary School

THE MAGIC WINDOW

There once was a very small window,
Hidden away in the corner of a room.

One day, a policeman looked through the window
And saw a peaceful country.

One day a burglar looked through the window
And saw a museum filled with clear diamonds and rings.

One day a queen peered through the window
And saw crystals, crowns and jewellery.

One day a schoolgirl looked through the window
And saw herself as a doctor working hard to help people.

One day a dwarf looked through the window,
And saw himself bigger than the mountains in Italy.

One day a ballet dancer glanced through the window
And saw herself performing to an audience, including the Queen.

One day God looked through the window
And the mirror smashed into tiny pieces.

Jessica Coombes (11)
Pen Y Fai CIW Primary School

MY WEEK

Monday, I always get up late,
Tuesday, I'm going on a date.
Wednesday, it is football,
Thursday, it is PE in the hall.
Friday, it is last day in school.
Saturday, the weekend off, that's cool.
Sunday, the end of another perfect week.

Jack Lewis (11)
Pen Y Fai CIW Primary School

FINGER

An eye poker,
A nose picker,
A button pusher,
A page turner,
A Subbuteo flicker,
A head scratcher,
An ear cleaner,
A rubber band stretcher,
A runny nose wiper,
A mini leg.

Matthew Hof (11)
Pen Y Fai CIW Primary School

LIFE

Life is a roller-coaster,
It has its ups and downs,
But you should enjoy the ride,
Before it ends forever.

Childhood is a Jack-in-the-box,
Full of good surprises,
With the unexpected fright,
But bringing happy times.

Marriage is a chain,
Once made, linked forever,
It must be protected from rust,
So that the chain is not broken.

Death is an open door
With a handle on one side,
You are forced through
Into a better life.

Rhian Jordan (11)
Pen Y Fai CIW Primary School

MONDAY'S HAIR

Monday's hair is flat and stiff,
Tuesday's hair has a big quiff,
Wednesday's hair is curly and groovy,
Thursday's hair is ready for the movies,
Friday's hair is over the top,
Saturday's hair looks like a mop,
Sunday's hair I must admit,
This style is really 'it'.

Ceri Philpott (11)
Pen Y Fai CIW Primary School

WINDOW

There once was a very small window
hidden away in the corner of a room.

One day a schoolboy peered through the window
and saw a pile of homework finished.

A prisoner glanced through the window
and saw the prison gates open.

A soldier glimpsed through the window
and saw aliens invading Earth.

A pop star peeped through the window
and saw his band winning Brit Awards 2000.

A mother looked through the window
and saw a clean baby's bottom.

A teenager looked through the window
and saw a life supply of beer.

A gardener peeked through the window
and saw a garden with no weeds.

I looked through the window
and saw a servant who tidied my bedroom.

Mark Borgia (11)
Pen Y Fai CIW Primary School

HURRICANE HANNAH VISITS THE ZOO

It dodged through the crowd,
It swayed between cages,
It ran past the keeper,
It went on for ages.

The hippo was angry,
The lion did roar,
The monkeys were laughing,
Asking for more.

The penguins a-flurry,
The bears did quake,
The giraffe shouted,
'Oh, for goodness sake!'

The snakes did shiver,
The otter did roll,
The poor little rabbit
Hid under his bowl.

The parrot did squawk,
The zebra went pale,
As the wind continued
To howl and wail.

The gorilla was frightened,
The apes were too,
The rhino didn't know
What to do.

The puma leaped
As the leopard pranced,
The crocodile snapped
While the flamingos danced.

The camel panicked,
The eagles flew,
The night sky
Turned to morning's blue.

The storm died,
Like an animal trapped,
Fighting to live
As the thunder clapped.

The rain fell,
The sun broke through,
Across the sky
A rainbow grew.

Rhiannon Pritchard (10)
Pen Y Fai CIW Primary School

WRAPPER

A sweet jacket,
A piece of colourful paper,
A rippable sheet,
An ingredients teller,
A bin filler,
A pocket fitter,
A folder upper,
A translucent plastic,
A mini parachute,
A plastic paper,
A pretty sheet,
A litter bug,
A recyclable item.

Alexander McColgan (11)
Pen Y Fai CIW Primary School

WHAT AM I?

A litter blower,
A leaf sucker,
A howl maker,
A big vacuum cleaner,
A car twister and tumbler,
A talented juggler,
A wall stripper,
A glass shatterer,
A sky scraper,
A tree bender,
A dust maker.
What am I?

A hurricane.

Martyn Mordecai (12)
Pen Y Fai CIW Primary School

I'D RATHER BE

I'd rather be a line than a dot,
I'd rather be a stripe than a spot,
I'd rather be a cradle than a cot,
I'd rather be a bow than a knot,
I'd rather canter than trot.

I'd rather be happy than sad,
I'd rather be good than bad,
I'd rather be sane than mad,
I'd rather be given than had,
I'd rather be mum than dad.

I'd rather be white than black,
I'd rather be a dog than a cat,
I'd rather be a bag than a sack,
I'd rather be Ben than Jack,
I'd rather a thump than a whack.

Helena Seward (11)
Pen Y Fai CIW Primary School

WINDOW

There was once a very small window,
hidden away in the corner of a room.

One day a young child looked through the window
and saw himself in a toy shop that belonged to him.

An old lady peered through the window
and saw all the good times she had in the past.

A gardener gazed through the window
and saw a field filled with flowers swaying in the breeze.

A prisoner looked through the window
and saw the gates opening to freedom.

The Undertaker looked through the window
and saw his fighting opponent on the floor, knocked out.

A footballer stared through the window
and saw his team winning the World Cup.

An inventor looked through the window
and saw what the year 3248 would be like.

I looked through the window
and I saw what my life will be like when I'm older.

But a ghost looked through the window
and saw what happened in his life.

Christopher Franklin (11)
Pen Y Fai CIW Primary School

GIRAFFE

Long-necker,
Leaf-eater
Tail-swinger,
Foot-thumper,
Fast-runner,
Hard-kicker,
Eye-flutterer,
Cute-lipper.

Yasmin Devi-McGleish (10)
Pen Y Fai CIW Primary School

MOUSE

Cheese nibbler,
Nose twitcher,
Tail shaker,
Secret hider,
Floor scurrier,
Furry friend,
Squeaky snorer,
Ear wiggler,
Cosy cuddler.

Rhian Thomas (10)
Pen Y Fai CIW Primary School

LET'S GO TO THE CIRCUS

Let's go to the circus and have some fun,
Candyfloss for everyone.
We watch the monkeys jumping around,
Then they suddenly fall to the ground.

The elephants are next on show,
On they come and bow down low.
On their back legs they stand up high,
Then they nearly reach the sky.

The clowns come on and do some tricks,
They mess around with loads of bricks.
The show has finished, so let's go home
And go to bed all alone.

Hannah Barrett (9)
St Clare's Preparatory School

SPRING

The cock is crowing,
The stream is flowing,
The flowers are growing,
The small birds twitter,
The lake will glitter,
The butterflies flying
And the sun is hinging.
The children are playing,
The trees are growing,
The cattle are grazing,
Their heads never raising,
The moon is growing,
The day is ending,
So everybody rests and sleeps.

Yasmin Cuddy (9)
St Clare's Preparatory School

TIGER

One day I saw a tiger
walking slowly by.
'Hello' I said, he turned his head
and looked me in the eye.

He stared and stared and stared at me,
my legs began to shake,
I quickly turned and ran away
and jumped into the lake.

Out I got and off I ran
as fast as fast could be,
before he ran to catch me up
and make a meal of me.

Joshua Williams (9)
St Clare's Preparatory School

THE TOOTH FAIRY

Once a tooth fairy came in my house,
She was really quiet, quiet as a mouse.
She crept upstairs in my room,
But then I woke up oh so soon!
I saw her standing on my bed,
'Who are you?' I suddenly said,
'I am the tooth fairy and I have come
For your tooth to take to fairy land.
So be a good girl and go to sleep
And I will put some money in your hand.
Now I will fly up in the sky,
So goodbye for now, because I must fly.'

Deanna Griffiths (8)
St Clare's Preparatory School

THE SNOWMAN

In winter it's cold
And the plants don't grow,
The sky turns white
And it starts to snow.
The children stay home from school this day,
They wrap up warm and go out to play.

Scarves, gloves, wellies and hats,
Children slide along on sledges and mats.
They run about and get wet and cry,
Their mums come out and make them dry.

The children start off with a snowball,
They roll it along until it is tall,
Then they make a smaller ball for his head,
It goes on his body, 'It looks good,' they said.

For his eyes they got two pieces of coal,
A carrot for his nose, they stuck in a hole.
For his mouth they drew a nice thick line,
Two sticks for arms, they looked like mine.

Next he wears a hat on top
And for his hair he wears a mop
A scarf he wears around his neck
Then along came a bird who gave him a peck.

The children build this big snowman
He looked so tall, as tall as a van
The snowman was fun and always silly
So the children called him Mr Chilly.

He stands around when it is cold
He watches children or so we are told
When it gets warm he melts away
'Goodbye Mr Snowman, see you again one day.'

Emily Robinson (9)
St Clare's Preparatory School

THE FRIENDLY DRAGON

The big green dragon
All full of smoke,
Chases the wagon
And makes people choke.

His name is Fig
And he lives in a cave,
He chews on a twig,
Oh, he doesn't know how to behave.

The people all love him,
They visit him every day
And his best friend Tim
Always shouts 'Hooray!'

Jordan Williams (8)
St Clare's Preparatory School

WINNIE THE WITCH

Winnie the Witch
Woke up one day,
She went outside
And flew away.

Winnie the Witch
Didn't go very far,
She flew into a ditch
And longed for a car.

Winnie the Witch
Cackles all day and all night,
But she only manages to
Give a mouse a fright.

Winnie's skin's white and warty,
Her nose long and hooked,
It shouldn't be hard
To make you quite spooked.

But the trouble with Winnie
Is she's not very good
At being a wicked old witch.
It's not in her nature
For people to hate her,
She's really a loveable creature.

Rhiannon Burridge (10)
St Clare's Preparatory School

LET'S NOT

Let's go out to play'
My little sister said.
'Let's not,' I replied.
'I'd rather go to bed!'

'Let's play Polly Pocket,'
She said with a grin.
'Really!' I said
'I'd rather sleep in the bin!'

'How about teddy bears' picnic?'
She said, 'With plastic beef pie.'
'Oh please,' I cried, 'Definitely not,
I'd rather die!'

Along comes Mum,
'How about some homework?' she said.
'Let's not,' we replied.
And away we went to bed.

Amy Barrett (11)
St Clare's Preparatory School

FIREWORKS

F ireworks are really pretty
I n the sky the shooting stars shine.
R ed, yellow, green and gold
E verywhere for us to see
W hirling Catherine wheels are lots of fun
O utside is where we all must be to see
R ockets flying, soaring high.
K ing-size Roman candles exploding
S parklers are my favourite treat
   especially when they crackle and glow.

Hannah Williams (10)
St Clare's Preparatory School

SCHOOL DINNERS

Sandwiches are full of yummy ham,
Cake is full of tart and jam.

Hungry children have lots to eat,
Oranges, apples are really not meat.

Other things are not really feasts,
Like cooked dinner with gravy, tender and sweet.

Drinks like Coke are really nice,
Ice-cream is sometimes as white as rice.

Never a day can we go without McDonald's,
Never a day can we go without their chips.

Every week we always go,
Riding in a van which is white and slow.

Sorry I have to go so soon but the food chart has finished,
Now I have to finish too!

Roshni M Patel (10)
St Clare's Preparatory School

WHAT'S IN THE SEA?

What's in the sea?
Fish swimming round and round.
What's in the sea?
Lovely brown sea horses.
What's in the sea?
Orange small starfish.
What's in the sea?
Grey dolphins jumping up and down.
What's in the sea?
A blue octopus.
What's in the sea?
A beautiful big whale.
What's in the sea?
Turtles swimming.
What's in the sea?
An electric eel.
What's in the sea?
A jellyfish.
What's in the sea?
Snapping crabs.
What's in the sea?
Beautiful green seaweed.
What's in the sea?
Oh, a man-eating shark!
What's in the sea?
I do not know, do you?

Nadia Nawaz (11)
St Clare's Preparatory School

THE CLOWN

The clown is always happy,
He is never a sad chappie.
He even wears brown,
And he always makes a loud sound.

He works in a circus,
With lots of other acts.
There is always a lot of sand and sawdust.
Going to the circus is a must.

Katie Owen (9)
St Clare's Preparatory School

My Rabbit

From the time when I was a very small boy,
I never was happy to play with a toy.
I nagged and I nagged and I asked for a pet,
But Mum always answered, 'Keep waiting, not yet!'

I waited and waited and when I was nine,
We went out to choose one and now she is mine.
She is fluffy and gentle and has lovely soft fur,
She jumps and she leaps and I think I love her.

She waits for my footsteps when I come through the gate,
And she thumps on her hutch if I'm a bit late.
The waiting was worth it for Graham and me,
Well, I didn't know that he was a she!

Alexander Burke (9)
St Clare's Preparatory School

The Flying Dreamer

I'd love to fly like a golden eagle,
And flap my graceful wings.
If I was a golden eagle,
I could do most anything.
The beak, oh, so beautiful and curved,
The talons are so sharp.
Oh the graceful golden eagle,
I adore with all my heart.

The eagle is my one true love,
It is really cool,
Oh I love it so much,
I would fight for it in a duel!
The eagle is loveable and strong,
Maybe I will fly one day
With the eagle high.
Yes I will fly one day in the pale blue sky.

Luke Karmali (10)
St Clare's Preparatory School

WORDS

Words! Words!
What do they do?
They help communication,
From me to you.

Words! Words!
Where do they come from?
They come from our pen,
Like the word, hen.

Words! Words!
Where do they come from?
They come from my head,
When I'm in bed.

Pauline Gallagher (9)
St Clare's Preparatory School

COMPUTERS

Computers are really fun,
Computers are for everyone.
Computers run on battery,
They also run on electricity.

Computers are very fast,
You can also play games on the PC.
Surfing the internet will surely last,
Computers are really cool.

Imran Khan (9)
St Clare's Preparatory School

THE RABBIT

My rabbit is called Suzy,
She is very nice.
She is always cuddly and loveable,
Her colours are black and white.

She likes to burrow in the soil,
And play on the grass.
She mostly hides in bushes,
And she is very fast.

It's hard to try and catch her,
No matter what you do.
You might just touch her lovely fur,
But still I love Sue!

Sally Krouma (9)
St Clare's Preparatory School

THE BEGINNING OF FREEDOM

As the time nears half-past three,
On the very last day of term,
I begin to feel the excitement,
And start wriggling like a worm.

As the bell goes, I jump with joy,
And I run out of the school.
A few weeks holiday is what I need,
In a hotel with a pool.

Sunshine, swimming, playing games,
Doing everything that is fun.
I will enjoy myself I know,
If no homework needs to be done.

Huw John (9)
St Clare's Preparatory School

MOBILE PHONES, COMPUTERS AND TELEVISIONS.

My phone is ringing,
And I'm in work,
My arm is stinging
I'm quite a jerk.

Computers are fun
But PlayStations are better.
Most people play on them,
In this nation.

Televisions are great,
There are cartoons on them.
But we cannot watch them,
When we are doing dictation.

Gareth Morgan (9)
St Clare's Preparatory School

OBSTACLE COURSE

The whistle blew, off I went,
I travelled through the ropes.
I squeezed through the tyres,
I swung from the trees,
Then crossing the stream without getting wet.

Under the nets,
Into the sacks, quick now squeeze in!
Over the tree trunk standing up
Please pull me up.

Kate Louise James
St Clare's Preparatory School

WHY?

Why can't I eat an ice-cream in the middle of the night?
Why do I get told off and Mum and Dad say I'm not right?
Why can't I scream and shout at work time in school?
Why can't I dive into the local swimming pool?
Why are the things that are good fun the things that I can't do?
Why can't I play netball when I've only got the flu?
Why do people call me a tomboy when I'm really as sweet as can be?
Why are lessons in school always as boring as a coconut on a tree?
Maybe Mum and Dad are right.
But why?

Emily Wood (9)
St Clare's Preparatory School

MY PET

It's funny my dog knows just how I feel,
If I feel bad,
You can tell how he feels,
His eyes are all sad.

It's funny my dog knows just how I feel,
If I feel happy,
You can tell how he feels,
His tail is all flappy.

It's funny my dog knows just how I feel,
If I feel happy or bad.
You can tell how he feels,
It's either a flappy tail or his eyes looking sad.

Lia Renkes (8)
St Clare's Preparatory School

RAINBOW

When rain and sun mix together,
A colourful arch comes,
Because of the weather.
People pass and see it in the sky,
So do the birds as they fly by.

At the end there's a pot of gold,
It gives us light the dark behold.
When the end of the day comes it starts to fade,
As if it's the cool, dark shade.

My favourite colour is the indigo
And also the blue.
The colour of the violets,
With a sky and a flying cuckoo.

As the day comes to an end,
You see no arch.
But you can still see it in any month,
February, June or March.

Lara Morris (8)
St Clare's Preparatory School

EYES

In the dark, the cats' eyes glare,
As they blink and as they stare.
Eyes when sad, cry salty tears,
And eyes grow wide especially with fears.

Eyes when glad, twinkle and shine,
Whether young or old, if ninety or nine.
Eyes are a gift from God to see,
The wonderful world he made for me.

Catherine Devine (9)
St Clare's Preparatory School

SCHOOL

I like to go to school,
Most of all because we have a pool.
It is cold but I don't care,
Because I like to swim in there.

Lunchtime and breaktime are very good,
We go down the field and pretend it's a wood.
My sister likes to play on the bars,
I am sure she thinks she's on planet Mars.

The bell rings and we run to line,
I am in the front and that is fine.
Up the stairs and into the class,
Mrs Pearce says, 'Spellings, I hope you all pass!'

Emma Louise Dean (8)
St Clare's Preparatory School

MY DOG

My dog is a hog,
He hogs the bathroom day and night,
He uses it to fly his kite.

I love my dog I do, I do!
Oh no, he has just blocked the loo!
Anyway he is quite sweet,
Except when he ate my parakeet.

Goodbye see you later!
Oh no, my dog has just been eaten by an alligator!

Jennifer Delemore (9)
St Clare's Preparatory School

PETS

Some people like cats that purr,
Not many people like cats that bite!
Some people like cats that go out at night.

Some people like dogs that play,
Not many people like dogs that bark!
Some people like dogs that sleep all day.

Some people like rabbits that run around,
Not many people like rabbits that make a mess!
Some people like rabbits that don't make a sound.

Lauren A Williams (8)
St Clare's Preparatory School

SKIING

I'm going on a holiday to ski far and wide,
Maybe I'll do some snowboarding along the hillside.
I'll have to buy a skiing suit and hire a pair of skis.
I'll probably go to skiing class and learn to bend my knees.
When I go to have my lunch it might be melted cheese.

I like to go fast,
I like to go quick,
But I have to be careful or else I'll slip.
When I get back there's time for a dip,
But then I'm off because I need some kip.

William Kinder (9)
St Clare's Preparatory School

COMMUNICATIONS

Mobile phones,
Oh mobile phones,
Buy them and you will see,
It is the key.

Televisions are the best,
For everyone to see.
Hope a comedy,
Is your speciality.
The things that you like,
Are there, not out of sight!

Mitul Jay Patel (9)
St Clare's Preparatory School

CARS

Cars here, cars there,
Cars are practically everywhere!
Lots of different colours too,
Red, green, white and blue.

Jaguar, Mercedes, Porsches and more,
All their engines give a tremendous roar.
Cars are very useful,
They'll help you when you're chased by a bull.

Amessh Patel (9)
St Clare's Preparatory School

LOST

I've landed and it's very big,
So many planets, probably about a hundred.
Jupiter, the sun and lots more.
Oh no, I've lost Adam and Richard,
Now what do I do?
I'm lost, alone,
And I've run out of fuel!

Now then how long are we going to be here?
Probably until the next Millennium.
I'll call on the radio.
Space rocket number ten - over!
We read - over!
I've run out of fuel on Jupiter - over!
Space refueller on his way - over!

At last lights are coming
At last we're safe.
Oh no, I think it's aliens!
Hello, we're the E G aliens
Have you got any fuel
Yes, I've put it in your space rocket.

Richard Raymond (10)
St John's School

LOST

Lost in a graveyard nowhere to go,
Bats flying everywhere.
Owls hooting, tu-whit tu-whoo.
Lost in a graveyard with hogs in bogs.
Lost in a graveyard, lightning crackling.
Birds and bats flapping and flying,
But don't be afraid just walk through those gates.
And you'll surely be saved.

Those gates are the first thing you see,
If you stare at it long enough.
It'll make you have a fright.
There are steel bars painted black,
Next to it there is a sack full of coal.
I took my first step and stepped on a mole.
The mole squealed in pain and said
'I'll hang your head with a crane'
So I followed the mole tunnel and it took me home.

Justin Davies (9)
St John's School

LOST

Lost at the North Pole nowhere to go.
Polar bears roaring,
Penguins squeaking,
Snow is cold.
Frostbite on my fingers and nose,
But don't be afraid, camp in the middle of nowhere,
Zip up your sleeping bag and make a fire.

Ground shaking, penguins crying, afraid of falling down a big hole.
Legs shaking on the ground
Ice cracking and breaking,
Legs freezing and slipping,
Food frozen is solid so you can't eat it.
But don't be afraid, don't freeze to death,
The doctor will be there to help.

Nathan Rogers (9)
St John's School

LOST

Lost in the Dome
Don't know where to go.
Acrobats in the air,
Can't see where.
Lots of people around you,
Don't know where,
Because you're so small there.

Lost in the Dome,
All I could hear was,
Ba-boom ba-boom ba-boom!
Ba-boom, ba-boom, ba-boom!
It was my heart beating,
Loud in the air.

I woke up the next morning,
All I had had was a dream . . .

Liane Thomas (8)
St John's School

LOST

Lost in the future,
Where in the new world?

In the sky are gold and silver flying cars,
Giant skyscrapers all around,
No pollution, no war going on.

People replaced by robots and computers,
No need to worry.

Medicine is so powerful we can live for over one hundred years,
But no need to look wrinkly, we don't need to look old,
People are lost in happiness, in the future world.

Laura Thomas (8)
St John's School

LOST

I was lost in a toy shop
I didn't know what to do.
Something grabbed onto my leg.
I screamed!
I ran and ran and then the toys began to chase me,
I was on my own.
All the toys were chasing me.
I was scared.
Everything went silent
I reached for the door, I made it.
But then my mum woke me up,
So then I knew it was a dream.

Rhys Llewellyn (8)
St John's School

LOST

I went to town to buy my kit,
I trained and trained and now I'm fit,
To take part in a special race,
And travel into outer space!

We had to make this trip alone,
But I took my mobile phone.
My little spaceship was called 2K,
We travelled through the Milky Way.

Round and round the moon I went,
I heard a bump - 2K was bent.
I was scared I tried to scream,
It woke me up - I've had a dream.

Christopher Hughes (8)
St John's School

LOST

Big buildings and classrooms,
I didn't know where to go.
My mummy and daddy just dropped me off,
I'm feeling very low.

I went to see my teacher,
She was nowhere to be found.
I looked upstairs and downstairs,
But there wasn't a sound.

I looked in the classroom,
And through the big door.
She was sitting in the office,
When I tripped over something on the floor.

Matron was gentle and kind,
She wiped away my tears.
She phoned my mummy straight away
And coloured all my fears.

Alexander Thomas (8)
St John's School

LOST AT SEA

A calm, quiet sea,
Suddenly moody weather came.
A flash of yellow light,
A roar from the sky.
Smash! On the side of our ship.
Down we went.
It was like a kingdom,
A pretty sight.
But then I knew I was lost.
Under the sea - lost!
No escape - lost!
Can't get out,
Lost! Lost! Lost!
Stuck way out,
I swam fast to the shore,
Finally I was out of the water.

Aaron Loveluck-Frank (9)
St John's School

LOST

Lost in a cave
Bats flapping
Water dripping
Icicles cracking
Muddy grounds
Pitch-black.
Then all of a sudden
I heard footsteps
Crunching through the muddy grounds
Could it be Mum?
I hope it is!

The footsteps are getting louder
Nearer and nearer
My heart starts to pound.
All of a sudden
The person shouts out my name,
Could it be Mum?
Yes it is!

Nathan Lewis (9)
St John's School

LOST

Lost in the dark woods
Owls hooting and swooping
In front of my face
Crackling of the leaves
Beneath my feet.

The flashing eyes of a fox
Hiding behind the tree
He fell into a steady stare
But he ran smoothly out of sight.

It became darker in the woods
I couldn't see a thing
All I could do now
Was feel my way round
I fell over a rock.

I heard the squirrels
Jump from tree to tree
One almost fell on me
But got caught on a branch.

All this started to scare me
I ran
I shouted for help
But nobody came
I ran around for a while
And I finally got out
I was safe.

Rhys Jones (8)
St John's School

LOST

Once I was lost in a cave
A deep, dark cave
With stalagmites
And stalactites
Sparkling up and down.

Once I was lost in a cave
A deep, dark cave
With gloomy creatures
Called terminites.

Once I was lost in a cave
A deep, dark cave
I screamed to help
But no one came
So that was the end of me.

Gareth Rhys Williams (9)
St John's School

LOST

Once I was lost in a jungle
            A lifeless jungle
No birds, no water nor fruit.

Once I was lost in a jungle
            A lifeless jungle
No sun, no moon nor stars.

Once I was lost in a jungle
            The life returned
I woke up from my dream
            My lifeless dream.

Nathan Hubbard-Miles (8)
St John's School

GRASS MOODS

When the wind blows I bend and feel cold.
When the rain pours I get wet and feel damp.
When the sun shines I am warm and regain my energy.

When the snow falls I perish and nearly die.
When the storm arises I blow around and break.

In the spring I feel happy and sometimes cold.
In the summer I feel refreshed, warm and sad.
In the autumn I feel horrible and angry.
In the winter I feel freezing.

Michael Hontoir (11)
St John's School

LOST IN SPACE

I felt a bubble soft and clear
It's my helmet
I walk into a gigantic rocket
A burning light fills the sight
The radio blares out words,
That means nothing to me,
Five
Four
Three
Two
One
I blast off in a gigantic rocket
And see the small rockets that surround me
Blast-off and blow up into the dark, dark space
I'm blasting through the spacey race
The radio blares out words
That means nothing to me
I'm lost in space
The spacey space
A crash! Bang! Wallop! what was that?
Wow! It happened so fast
I'm on the moon
White as snow.
      Oh no!
           How am I going to get back?

Owain Hume (9)
St John's School

LOST IN THE SUPERMARKET

Lost, lost
Where's Mum?
What was that?
I turned around
Two giant shelves towering over me
No ordinary shelves -
These were like ravishing lions!
Everything seemed alive.
Checkouts were snapping like crocodiles
Manager, glaring and staring
Like the Demon Headmaster.
Run! Run!
Run for your life
Past the peas,
Past the corn,
Past the bacon.
Bang! Mum!
We ran
We ran so fast
We broke the 100 metre record
The doors were shutting
We jumped -
Got outside -
Gasping for breath
I said 'I'm never going there again.'

Lewis Jones (9)
St John's School

LOST IN AN OCEAN

Deeper and deeper I dived
Down to the ocean bed
Tiny fish spread
Across the ocean bed.

Swimming swiftly
Drifting slowly
For one hour or two
Maybe I went a mile
Or even two.

I turned back
Swam and swam
Different turnings
Which way did I come?
Which way shall I go?

Up to the surface
Nothing in sight.

Thomas Cooke (9)
St John's School

FIRE MOOD

I'm nothing but a flicker
Gazing at the sky
But soon I'll be a whopper
You'll see, I'll fly.

But the more I try
I find I'm turning black, fading away
Please help me, I'm nearly ash.

Some stupid soul
Threw a newspaper at me
Here I go, I'm on a roll.

I've scorched the rubbish bin
Burning the back garden
I'm near the house.

I jump and I tiptoe closer and closer
But what's this? My worst enemy *appears*!
Water, I've been sprayed by *water*.
I'm nothing but ash
Going, going, going, gone.

Andrew Beaven (11)
St John's School

MOODS

Envy is green
As green as the summer trees
Swaying in the breeze in the park.

Angry is red
As red as a hot coal-burnt fire
As red as your blood.

Loneliness is blue
As blue as the sky above us
As blue as the shallow Bahamas waters.

Happiness is yellow
Like the sun's morning rays
That always beats the rainy days.

Fiona Davies (11)
St John's School

MOODS OF A DOG

Happy moods of a dog are:
Bouncing and jumping
Racing and chasing
Barking at a frightful cat.

Angry dog moods are heckles rising
Growling viciously
Ready to attack.

A sleep dog mood is quiet
Gently drifting off
Peacefully dreaming of bones.

John Ladbrooke (11)
St John's School

Moods

An angry mood is burning red,
Like fire burning bright.

An envious mood is sickly green,
It's wanting everything else.

A jealous mood is dark, dark mauve,
It thinks that life's not fair.

A quiet mood is calm and tranquil,
It's colour is mostly turquoise.

A dreamy mood is never quite alert,
It's misty blue and very pale.

An adventurous mood is always restless,
It wants to explore the world.

Freya Michaud (11)
St John's School

MOODS

A silvery train that glows in the dark has a happy mood,
An erupting volcano that sprays lava has an angry mood,
A sleepy village near the sea has a lonely mood,
A deserted wood at midnight has a scary mood.

A snail that carries its house on his back has a slow mood,
White planes with red and blue stripes can have an angry mood,
But then they just fall out of the sky,
Just like a conker falling off a tree.

Green bushes at the end of the garden can have a dreamy mood,
Raging storms can have a mad mood,
A breaking down car can have an angry mood,
But sometimes they're just nice and calm.

Concorde airborne has a fast mood,
Speeding along at 1,000 mph,
Taking off in America,
Landing in Heathrow.

Jacob Clark (10)
St John's School

DIFFERENT MOODS

When you're sad,
You want to be alone,
To think things through.

When you're in a kind mood,
You feel considerate to others,
Helping anyone who's hurt.

When you're in a happy mood,
You like to do exciting things,
Like playing with your friends.

When you're in a quiet mood,
You like to sit in the summer sun,
To relax, read and write.

When you're excited,
You're running around,
Just like a steamboat.

A spiteful mood,
Is a cold, frosty,
Icy morning.

Charlotte Dibden (10)
St John's School

THE INVENTION

My mum always made me walk the dog
Even when I didn't want to
So I made an invention
It was called
The amazing dogwalker!
I tried a battery
Put in another, another and another,
'Bup! Beep! Dog-walker!' it said.

This is a dog-walker,
He doesn't do much.
He's plugged into the wall
Most of the time.
He only wakes up when it's
Time to do duty.

This dog-walker fits through the dog flap
My dog-walker's head rolls
Back and forth, back and forth
Because of that
He thinks he's a beauty.

My dog-walker is cool
To exercise a dog
He uses netting or the invention lead
It throws the ball
The dog runs after it!
My dog-walker is really cool.

Geraint Thomas (10)
St John's School

MOODS

Good moods, bad moods
Ill moods, sad moods.

Good moods are full of joy,
When you are playing with a toy.

Good moods, bad moods
Ill moods, sad moods.

Bad moods are full of sorrow,
When you're in one, you can't wait till tomorrow.

Good moods, bad moods
Ill moods, sad moods.

Ill moods are full of boredom,
When you've got a really sore tum.

Good moods, bad moods
Ill moods, sad moods.

Sad moods are full of despair,
You really feel that you don't care.

Harry Case (11)
St John's School

A MERMAID'S MOOD

My mood is filled
with colours
flashing by my side.
My hair whipping my back
With stings of harmless pride.
Wind pouring on my body
Making my eyes go
cold.
This mood is fast
Yet it feels
bold.
My fin has grown gradually
but my life is very
sure.
My mood is one colour . . . blue,
blue as the sea which is what
I live in.

Hannah Cooke (11)
St John's School

THE INVENTION - THE KEEP-YOU-CLEANER

The alarm goes off but I snuggle back down
But the bed tips over and all in a flash
I'm on the machine . . .
Mum says I've got to be clean!
I'm on the conveyor belt oh, oh, here we go
Through the cold shower burr!
I hate those hands that scrub your hair
Oh no, my ears are popping
Help me I'm not stopping.
Oh no here comes the toothpaste and brush
Now it's time for the hair comb.
I'm in a rush!
Now it's time to get dressed
Why did my mum invent this machine?
But the good, the good thing about it is
It only takes thirty seconds
And you're never late for school.

Katherine Stevens (10)
St John's School

THE INVENTION

A walking suitcase would come in handy
To all you shopaholics,
So that you can give your arms a rest
And jump around and frolic.

Well that is my invention,
That I made just overnight,
I made it with a hammer and nails,
When I finished, it looked quite a sight.

It looked like a treasure chest,
That a pirate dug up,
It has hard, harsh wood,
Made of Bomcabup.

I took it to the shopping mall,
And it gobbled up my food.
It ate the lady at the counter,
In the end it got me sued.

He swallowed a man,
And his dog,
He ate a pram,
He burped and out came fog!

All was misty,
You couldn't see a thing,
Apart from dust
And something that came out of a bin!

The thing with this wood is it stretches,
It can fit almost anything in its belly,
But it is allergic to one thing . . .
A great, big bowl of jelly!

I gave him jelly,
He ate it up,
All of a sudden, he started to hiccup.
He coughed everyone up,
But I still have that bill,
Next I think I'll make a . . .
Money Machine!

Rebecca Williams (10)
St John's School

THE INVENTION: THE NON-POLLUTING PLANE

It's a wonder plane,
It flies like a dream.
It goes very fast,
It stays very clean.
It's got a swimming pool
And an arcade too.
If you want to come for a ride
Please let us take you!
We'll take you to the country
You want to go too
Just let us know when
And we'll take you!

Vincent Chan (9)
St John's School

THE INVENTION

My computer reads my mind,
It leaves all the others far behind.
You can write on the screen even if you're blind.
That's my computer.

Put the patch to your neck,
Click on the words, it'll do a spellcheck.
Like brand new computers and mobile phones,
I can make my computer sing in different tones.
That's my computer.

If you want to change the colour or the font,
You have to enter a password which no one will get.
You can bank online,
You can shop online
You can even send your mail.
You can book your tickets for aeroplanes
You can get tickets to go by rail.

An invention of the future, I should say,
It will cost so much.
Only rich people will pay
So what do you think,
Will it be true?
If it is, I'll make this computer
Just for you.

Alexandros Antonopoulos (9)
St John's School

THE INVENTION

My dad bought my mum the most
amazing present for her birthday,
It was made in January 2000
It's called a Holiday Simulator!
Your house can be anything,
A restaurant with a delicious menu.

It doesn't take long to build
You could go to Disneyland
To see Mickey Mouse
All in your house!

But I didn't do any of those things
Because my dad didn't read the instructions!

When he plugged it in boom! Bash!
The kitchen was a hotel room!
My room was a zoo
And don't ask me what the bathroom was
My dad's room was a golf course.

It was cool because I had a tiger
The school bullies stopped bullying me
My English teacher didn't give me any prep!

But some engineers came and fixed the problem
And guess what happened?
I don't have my pet any more
So I get detention!

Thomas Arthur (9)
St John's School

THE INVENTION

The pen with life!
The best pen in the world!
You can buy them in the Invention Shop.
£30,000 you can buy them
In red, blue, black, yellow.
The ink colour is blue, black, red, green.
Come down to the Invention Shop
With your money
Now!
Good for teachers and children
Who get handaches,
Good for teachers who have
A lot of marking to do.

It runs on electric
It is hard so if it falls off the table
It won't break.
It has a wheel at the bottom so it can move itself
And can stand up alone.
The box at the top is the bit you speak into
Tell it what to do
It writes for you!

James Greenway (10)
St John's School

THE INVENTION

The invention has the intention,
To change life on Earth,
An automated *real* clock,
Should be in an invention shop.

Which is the best, what will it be?
An automated *real* clock,
Is the best you'll see!

Press a few buttons, what will you see?
It could be a mountain or it could be a tree,
Time travel, that's what it is,
Flick the hands back and you're
Back where you were . . .

Of course there's a time limit,
In case of danger and if someone
Sees you, the clock will hide you away.

What if you think a clock is too big?
Watches!

I turned the left knob,
And then the right knob,
Off I went.
Flash, pop, bang,
I was falling from the sky,
And I landed flat and dry.
A sandstorm was raging,
And I was quickly ageing,
Quickly turn the knob,
Bang, pop, flash
I was back in my own time.

Oliver Battrick (10)
St John's School

THE INVENTION: THE ROBOTIC MOTHER

My invention is a cunning plan,
Very mischievous,
It likes a lot of weird things,
The favourite food is ham.

She will help Mum,
Night and day.
Then she tells us
She needs recharging 'Batteries please.'

It will do the hoovering,
Dry and wash up,
Don't forget polishing,
And it is best at cooking.

It has purple eyes
And wears a wig.
It likes the blue shawl it wears
On a Friday night.

If the robot wasn't there,
I would be a replacement.
Even if it is hard work
Being a cleaner.

Chantellé Coleman (8)
St John's School

ROBO ARM

My invention is the Robo Arm,
'A Robo Arm!' my friend said,
When I rang him in my bed.
It is big, it is hard
and it is very, very large.
I invented it in the year 2000.

'Hello machine that organises my school bag!'
'Master! Have a hug!'
I got dressed,
But I forgot to put on my vest!
'Come on Robo Arm!' I said
'Robo Arm reporting for duty!'
'Fly, fly take me to school!'
'Yes master, yes master' said the Robo Arm.

Whew, we were at school
He called me a silly fool!
And took books from everybody's lockers
He did my work and when the teacher marked it
They were all wrong.

After school I stamped up the stairs
In a crash, bang, bang mood,
'Can I be of assistance?' the Robo Arm said
'Remember, age before beauty'
'Robo Arm reporting for duty!'
Bang! Robo Arm plopped from the window.

Matthew Perkins (10)
St John's School

MRS PUSSY THE ROBO MUM

One rainy afternoon
I got very, very bored.
I decided to make an invention
I was so excited
I stood up and roared.

My invention is called Mrs Pussy
She's very, very sweet
She does all the cooking and washing
I don't understand how she's so neat.

Mrs Pussy can turn into a car
The coolest car in town
She's even got a sweet machine
And she's got a bar!
But I'm not allowed to use it
Because there's alcohol
Sometimes the car embarrasses me
Cos it's pink like a Barbie Doll.

When it comes to relaxation
Leave it to Mrs Pussy
She can turn into a jacuzzi
A pool or a sauna
Anything you like, use your imagination!

Bethan Llewellyn (11)
St John's School

THE MILKY MOO-COW

I have a cow and it is called
The Milky Moo-Cow.
He is four years old.
He walks backwards and forwards
And also sideways!
The colour of his skin is black and white.
Sometimes he gets scared in the night!
I made him in California in the sauna.
When I made him I became pasta
My mum and dad think he's boring.
I am going to sell him,
For about four hundred pounds!
The handy thing is that he makes me shake.
My cow makes milkshakes.
You pour the milk down his mouth and turn him on!
When he has counted to three
It all comes in my bowl.
If you want flavoured milkshake
You pour coloured milk in his mouth.
My favourite is lemon and lime.
He eats all the grass in four minutes fast
So my dad does not have to mow the lawn.

Jessica Roach (10)
St John's School

THE INVENTION

This is the new design of a car,
Beats the others by far.
It has a TV, video player and a Sega Dreamcast,
Better than the cars from the past.

The colour of the car is black
It's really fast on a racing track.
It breaks the record of the fastest time,
I feel so proud that the medal is mine.

It makes hot chocolate and has a cookie machine
It whips up cappuccino covered in cream.
On the front it has double flashlights,
So you can see better in the night.

It can travel at the speed of sound
It can dig a hole underground.
Its seats transform into armchairs,
The boot widens to make room for spares.

When it jumps off the pier
You can see dolphins very near
The fish are swimming all around you,
Oh! the sharks come, what do I do?

You can buy it for around 50,000 pounds
That's the cheapest price you can get around.
Buy it in the best car stores
If you pay double you get even more.

Ryan James (10)
St John's School

THE TRAVEL POD

It'll carry you anywhere!
To Tesco's, Sainsbury's or even Waitrose.
If you don't like shopping
It'll take you to the Odeon.
It is round, see-through, electric,
Seats that go up and down
With buttons for controls.
It hovers one to eight metres high.
It cuts through air space
At supersonic speeds.
Made from futuristic fibre
With its flexible, mechanical arms.
It will carry your shopping
From the Adidas, Reebok or Nike store.
And after a busy day out
It'll carry you back
To your warm, cosy bed
And before you know it
ZZZZZZZZZZZZZZZ

Charles Hoey (9)
St John's School

The Brainbuster Invention

I'm going to finish something brill by next week
Through and through lots of books I seek.
Looking for bits and bobs
I get the screwdriver to turn all the knobs.

After one year, two months, three weeks,
And four days it is done.
I'm really worn out.
Sometimes I'm so stressed
My hair is nearly torn out.

My Brainbuster thinks for you
It tells you what you should do.
Hands come out and do your work,
While you just sleep.

If you insult it, it will cry and weep!
It has really got a brain.
It really wants to be in showbiz
All it desires is lots of fame.

It's a hat you put upon your head
It's really comfy so you can wear it to bed.
It switches brains, his and yours
So when your mother asks you
He does all the chores!

But it's really very happy
Just at home with me
If I didn't have him
I don't know where I'd be!

Olivia Case (9)
St John's School

BUTTERFLY PARTY

One bright morning, I saw a butterfly
It was blue, pink, purple and red,
It was wearing an orange cloa,
I asked 'Where are you going?'
It said 'I'm going to the butterfly party, bye bye.'

Later on I saw a swarm of bees,
They were black and yellow,
Their tails were decorated,
They were decorated with paint.
They said they were also going to the butterfly party.

After the bees had left I saw a caterpillar,
Blue and green, dancing and jumping around,
He had a red nose and looked like a caterpillar clown,
I asked 'Are you going to the butterfly party?'
The answer was 'Yes, bye.'

Rebekah Jones (8)
Tynewydd Junior School

A LADYBIRD

A ladybird is a beautiful thing
It's awful sad it won't sing.
When they fly in the sky,
They think they're flying very high.
When they have babies,
They're sure to feel lazy.
A ladybird is a beautiful thing
It's awful sad it won't sing.

Hannah Jones
Tynewydd Junior School

THE JABBERWOCKY

As in deep thought stood
The bear with eyes of flame
Came rushing through the dark wood
And burbled as it came.
One! Two! One! Two! And through and through
The mighty back went snicker-snack!
He left it dead and with its head
He went rushing back.
And have you killed the bear?
Come to me my handsome boy!
Oh lovely day, hip, hip, hooray
He chortled in his joy.

Thomas Parry
Tynewydd Junior School

AUTUMN

Autumn's mood is cold and mellow,
He wears crispy, leafy hair!
Autumn is clothed in mouldy pants, groovy vest.
Autumn's breakfast is gone-off fish
He breathes gone-off slugs!
Mouldy leaves and rivers called Autumn
'Dad'
Autumn hates icy Jack Frost
Autumn just wants Prince Charles.

Zoe Perry (9)
Tynewydd Junior School

SUMMER

Summer is calm and cheerful,
She has shining, sparkling hair.
Summer wears shining, shimmering, shades.
She enjoys a meal of a red rocket lolly.
Summer's breath is spicy.
Summer's children are sun and rain.
Summer's enemy is winter
Summer wants to have summer all year.

Adam Warner
Tynewydd Junior School

SUMMER

Summer is happy when its sunny
Summer is cheerful and forgetful
She has dangerous, dazzling hair.
Summer wears slimy, suncream
She enjoys a meal of red hot-curry.
Summer's breath is hot and spicy
Summer's children are the sun and moon
Summer's enemy is lightning
Summer wants to be a pop star.

Chelsea O'Neill (10)
Tynewyddd Junior School

SUMMER

Summer is joyful and calm
She has glittery, golden hair.
Summer wears a golden dress!
She enjoys a meal of icy ice lollies
Red and melon flavour.
Summer's breath is minty
Summer's children are the sea and the beach
Summer's enemy is winter
Summer wants to have summer all the time.

Laura Evans (8)
Tynewydd Junior School

MY POEM OF A WORM

I once saw a wiggly worm
It jumped into the sky
It got stuck on a satellite
And turned into a butterfly.
I thought it was very pretty
With black and white spots
But when it came to dying
It just went Pop!

Steven P
Tynewydd Junior School

SEASONS

Spring is such a wonderful time,
Coloured flowers grow in a line,
Baby lambs are born
And fields are full of corn.

Summertime I like best,
Birds have babies in their nest,
I have so much fun
Getting brown in the sun.

Autumn time the leaves all fall
Which makes the trees look ever so tall,
Autumn time is not too hot
So Mum makes lots of stew in the pot.

Wintertime I really don't like
It's much to cold to go out on my bike.
I like to build a snowman in the snow
But it's so cold cos the north wind does blow.

Jazay Howells (8)
Tynewydd Junior School

SUMMER

Summer is happy, excited
She has golden glittery hair
Summer wears wet bathers!
She enjoys a meal of drippy-droppy
Chocolate ice-cream.
Summer's breath is hot.
Summer's children are a bucket and
A Spade.
Summer's enemy is winter
Summer wants to be the queen.

Natalie John (9)
Tynewydd Junior School

SUMMER

Summer is excited and cheerful,
She has long glistening hair
Summer wears a yellow dress!
She enjoys a meal of wibbly wobbly jelly
Summer's breath is cool moon mint
Summer's children are moon and stars
Summer's enemy is snowflakes
Summer wants to destroy the snow flakes.

James Davies (9)
Tynewydd Junior School

ONCE...

Once in a field,
So wide and long,
I saw a most wonderful
Creature,
That I ever saw.
It flew so high,
And danced in the sky,
So high above,
Just like an aeroplane
The beautiful colours,
The wonderful dance,
So long ago.
It danced on the corn,
Across the glistening lake,
Across the field,
So wide and long.

Scott Greenslade (9)
Tynewydd Junior School

AND BURBLED AS IT CAME

One two, one two and through and
Through. The blood bursting sword
Went snick-snack!
And left it dead and with its
Head he went singing back

And have you killed the monster?
Come to my arms my famous boy!
Oh happy day, hooray, hooray!
He chortled in his joy.

'Twas brilliant and slithery toads
Did swim and swim in the water
All scaly were the toads
And the moody gnats outgrew.

Sasha Webber (8)
Tynewydd Junior School

SUMMER

Summer is calm and cheerful
She has shiny golden hair
Summer wears fashionable flip-flops!
She enjoys a meal of burning hot bacon.
Summer's breath is cool.
Summer's children are the moon and the stars.
Summer's enemy is lightning.
Summer wants to get married.

Annie Davies
Tynewydd Junior School

BUGS

There were bugs all different kinds
Always looking for their behinds
They would be glad
But they are sad
But now they're mad!

There were two butterflies,
With bright coloured wings,
Just fluttering by
To say 'Hi'.

I love bugs, so many kinds
I think they're better than the
Wriggly kind!
Butterflies are beautiful with their wings,
They can do so many things!

Sarah Graham (9)
Tynewydd Junior School

SEA FEVER

I must go down to the seas again,
Where the grey, stormy sky awakes
As it casts its magic spell.
The thundering black sea clashes like thick
Frothy spume swishing,
While the horrified, frightened fish fly deep
Down under,
And all I ask is a glimpse of the brightened sun
Streaming through the moody, wintry clouds.
Because all I need to guide me home is a shimmering
Breeze and a glorious blue sky.

Nicola Baker (10)
Tynewydd Junior School

SEA FEVER

I must go down to the smooth seas again,
Where the grey, stormy sky separates
And dolphins go up to the fresh surface to do
Their amazing diving acrobatics,
With all the colourful fish swimming merrily
Along beneath them.
I need to see the sparkling orange sun,
Shining on the calm, steady ocean,
And all I ask is the white, fluffy clouds
To make the clear blue sky stand out.
I don't want the ugly, miserable grey clouds to
Come,
It makes the day very dim indeed!
At the end of the day I desperately need,
A shining north star to lead me back home!

Tomos Edwards (9)
Tynewydd Junior School

SEA FEVER

We must go down to the shore tonight to
watch the moonlit sky;
And everywhere I look and go the stars will
steer me by.
The blustery wind that blows the shore
had blown our ship off course.
The beautiful whales that sail the sea saved
our ship from harm.
So we, the sailors of the night are grateful
just once more.
To the whales who saved our lives
with courage to the blue.

Daniel Townsend (9)
Tynewydd Junior School

FIREWORKS

I hate fireworks
With their spine-chilling sparkles,
And their ballistic bangers,
And their flaming frightening fountains,
Yes, I hate fireworks.

Spine-chilling!
Frightening, flaming!
Smokin', sizzling, sparkling!
Shooting, spectacular!
Spine-chilling!

Zoe Wilkinson
Tynewydd Junior School

SAND TIGER POEM

I drew a sand tiger in the sand,
Using just my bare pink hand,
All was done on the beach,
Where it was out of reach,
He could eat only yellow,
It's a lovely colour, bold but
Rather mellow.

Leonie Hill (9)
Tynewydd Junior School

WIZARDS

I love wizards
With their magical, powerful
And their bright, spine-chilling
And their majestic, magical.
Yes, I love wizards.

Sam Hughes
Tynewydd Junior School